NAT TURNER'S SLAVE REBELLION IN AMERICAN HISTORY

Judith Edwards

Enslow Publishers, Inc.

40 Industrial Road	PO Box 38
Box 398	Aldershot
Berkeley Heights, NJ 07922	Hants GU12 6BP
USA	UK

http://www.enslow.com

Library of Congress Cataloging-in-Publication Data

Edwards, Judith, 1940–
    Nat Turner's slave rebellion in American history / Judith Edwards.
        p.   cm. — (In American history)
    Includes bibliographical references (p.) and index.
    Summary: A biography of the slave and preacher who, believing that
God wanted him to free the slaves, led a major revolt in 1831.
    ISBN 0-7660-1302-2
    1. Turner, Nat, 1800?–1831 Juvenile literature. 2. Southampton
Insurrection, 1831 Juvenile literature. 3. Slaves—Virginia—Southampton
County Biography Juvenile literature. [1. Turner, Nat, 1800?–1831.
2. Slaves. 3. Afro-Americans Biography. 4. Southampton Insurrection,
1831.] I. Title. II. Series.
F232.S7E39   2000
975.5'503'092—dc21
[B]   99-16687
                                                         CIP

Printed in the United States of America

10 9 8 7 6 5 4 3 2 1

To Our Readers: All Internet addresses in this book were active and appropriate
when we went to press. Any comments or suggestions can be sent by e-mail to
Comments@enslow.com or to the address on the back cover.

Illustration Credits: Enslow Publishers, Inc., pp. 60, 75, 91; Library of
Congress, pp. 11, 13, 17, 18, 20, 39, 56; National Archives, p. 94;
North Carolina Division of Archives and History, Raleigh, pp. 21, 22,
24, 29, 31, 36, 44, 45, 51, 77, 83, 86, 92; Reproduced from the
Dictionary of American Portraits, Published by Dover Publications, Inc.,
in 1967, pp. 70, 89.

Cover Illustration: Library of Congress; North Carolina Division of
Archives and History, Raleigh.

★ CONTENTS ★

*B*LOOD! *BLOOD!!*
BLOOD!!!
Another Insurrection!
    North Carolina is thrown into a high fever! The Avenger is abroad, scattering desolation and death in his path! . . . *At the last accounts, the insurgents were slaying and burning all before them, and women and children were flying in every direction almost distracted.* . . .

INSURRECTION

    We have no room for particulars—not even for comments. So much for oppression! so much for the happiness of the slaves! so much for the security of the South! Where now are our white boasters of liberty? . . . MEN MUST BE FREE!*[1]

—William Lloyd Garrison, *The Liberator*, September 24, 1831

The Richmond Troop arrived here this morning a little after 9 o'clock, after a rapid, hot and most fatiguing march from Richmond. On the road . . . we found the whole country thoroughly alarmed; every man armed, the dwellings all deserted by the white inhabitants, and the farms most generally left in possession of the blacks. On our arrival at this village, we found . . . Jerusalem . . . crowded from its foundation; for besides the considerable military force assembled here, the ladies from the adjacent country, to the number of 3 or 400, have sought refuge from the appalling dangers by which they were surrounded.

Here for the first time, we learnt the extent of the insurrection, and the mischief perpetrated. Rumor had infinitely exaggerated the first, swelling the numbers of the negroes to a thousand or 1200 men, and representing its ramifications as embracing several of the adjacent counties . . . but it was hardly in the power of rumor itself, to exaggerate the atrocities which have been perpetrated by the insurgents: . . . How, or with whom, the insurrection originated, is certainly not known. . . .[2]

—John Hampden Pleasants, the Richmond *Whig*, August 25, 1831

It was early dawn on Monday, August 22, 1831. From small farm to plantation in the densely wooded, rolling countryside of southeastern Virginia, into the border country of North Carolina, no one was asleep. Runners pelted into barnyards, yelling warnings. Doors were flung open. Families grabbed infants and horses and headed for the little town of Jerusalem. The county seat of Southampton County was itself only a village, cut from the woods like the other crossroads villages in this countryside surrounded by swampland.

Rumors flew that an army of twelve hundred slaves had revolted and was killing every white person it came upon. The local militia formed and began killing every black person it found. Panic and hysteria were the only plans of action. What had happened? Who was responsible for what the terrified slave owners believed was a massive, unstoppable slave revolt?

*A*bout the last of August came in a dutch man of warre [war] that sold us twenty Negars [Negroes]."

—John Rolfe, a tobacco planter and husband of the famed Pocahontas, recorded this sentence in his daily journal of events in early Jamestown, Virginia.[1] The year was 1619.

2

THE PECULIAR INSTITUTION

Slavery in America

Thus began slavery on the continent of North America. Jamestown was only twelve and a half years old in 1619, having been founded by 104 men and boys in the spring of 1607.

The colony started out with indentured servants, people who worked as unpaid employees for a certain number of years to pay for their trip to America. At first, these indentured servants were white, then both white and black. For blacks, the indenture system gradually evolved into slavery. Laws became different for black slaves and white indentured servants. In 1640, three indentured servants ran away. One, John Punch, was black. The other two, originating from Scotland and Holland, were white. The white servants were whipped and had a year added onto their original indenture time. John Punch was whipped and the court decreed that he "shall serve his said master or his assigns for the time of his natural Life here or elsewhere."[2] Punch became a slave.

By 1661, slavery was fully evolved in Jamestown. Blacks became persons who could not be punished by time added to their time of service. They were "incapable of making satisfaction by addition of time," because they were already serving life sentences.[3] A law passed in 1664 held that a white woman who married a slave had to serve the slave's master as long as the husband was alive. In addition, any children born to the couple must serve that master until they were thirty years old.

Virginia's way of dealing with the now established institution of slavery became the guideline for all the other colonies, and by 1700, there were no more white indentured servants in Virginia. By 1775, slaves formed one sixth of the population of the colonies on the mainland of North America.

Origins of the Peculiar Institution

Slavery is, indeed, a peculiar institution. Today, the idea of owning another human being seems far-fetched and almost unbelievable. Slavery, however, has almost always existed. In ancient times, slaves were the product of war. A conquering army brought back captives from the plundered country to serve as slaves. French writer Alexis de Tocqueville wrote about the institution of slavery, comparing slavery in the eighteenth and nineteenth centuries to slavery in ancient history: "The slave, amongst the ancients, belonged to the same race as his master, and he was often the superior of the two in education and instruction. Freedom was the only distinction between them."[4] Ancient slaves were often awarded their freedom and became contributing members of the society in which they had been slaves.

New World slavery began in the early 1400s. A Portuguese explorer named Goncalvez brought ten Negroes from the west coast of Africa to Lisbon, to prove he had really been to Africa. In ten years, there was an active African slave trade, centered in Lisbon. By the 1500s, other European countries, including England, interrupted the Portuguese trade monopoly and were active in the slave trade.

Most of the slaves were from an area in Africa that runs from the Senegal River to present-day Portuguese Angola. This slave traffic, which destroyed whole communities and civilizations, included people from many different cultures, speaking different languages and having different shapes, sizes, occupations, and ways of farming.

Often native chiefs traded people for needed goods such as cookware and textiles. The going rate was around $60 (around $600 today) for one healthy male slave.[5] Estimates of how many of its strongest, healthiest people Africa lost in the approximately four centuries of active slave trade range from 24 million to 60 million. For every slave who survived the forty-day voyage across the Atlantic Ocean, called "The Middle Passage," five died.

Most Africans were first sent to the West Indies, a series of islands located to the south and east of the United States. There, they worked in the sugarcane fields for around three years. If they survived, they were then sent to the English colonies on the mainland to be sold. Slavery was introduced in all of the colonies, not just in the South.

As soon as slavery took hold, so did the desire of slaves to protest their unwanted position. To prevent uprisings, slave codes were passed by the colonies. South Carolina published a slave code in 1712 that had thirty-five sections. It was referred to as "An Act for the better ordering and governing of Negroes and Slaves."[6]

Slaves were not needed as much in the middle colonies because more white laborers had immigrated to colonies such as New York. In 1740–1741, New York, with the largest northern slave population, suffered a terribly severe winter. Everyone was affected, especially poor people and slaves. New Yorkers were afraid that the slaves would help Spain in a war, called "The War of Jenkins's Ear," part of a series of European political wars that Spain was fighting with England. Panic and hysteria erupted over a series of fires of unknown origin on February 28, 1741, because it was believed that the fires were part of a giant slave plot. Sentencing was harsh. Of the 150 persons involved, all but 25 were black slaves.

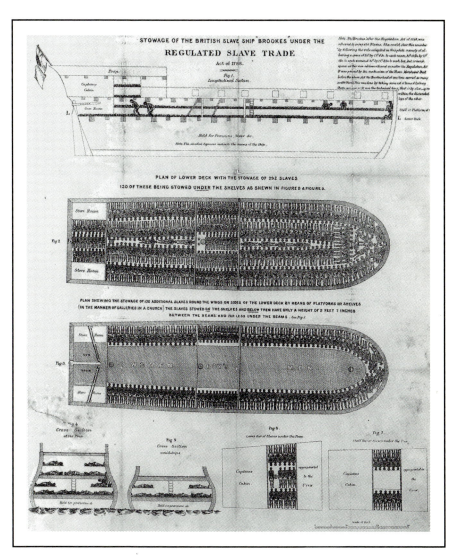

African slaves were brought to America on ships, crammed together with barely enough room to move. This drawing shows the floor plan of a slave ship, indicating how slaves would be transported.

Early Protests Against Slavery

Protests by white groups began shortly after the slaves arrived. In 1688, the Quakers, a religious group made up of people who are against war and all kinds of intolerance, spoke out against slavery. In a historic document called the Germantown Protest, the Quakers gave reasons why human beings should not be enslaved:

> There is a saying that we shall do to all men like as we will be done ourselves; making no difference of what generation, descent or colour they are, and those who steal or rob men, and those who buy or purchase them, are they not all alike? Here is liberty of conscience, which is right and reasonable; here ought to be likewise liberty of the body. . . . But to bring men hither, or to rob and sell them against their will, we stand against.[7]

Quakers continued to protest, as did many in the New England colonies.

A slave named Jenny Slew, of Ipswitch, Massachusetts, brought suit and was awarded her "freedom and four pounds for past labors."[8] Phillis Wheatley, a slave born in Africa, was the first black woman in colonial America to publish a book of poems. She was treated as one of the family by her masters, but still wrote movingly about her innermost wish—freedom.

Slavery During the American Revolution

Called the decade of discontent, the years between 1765 and 1775 saw a widening rift between Great

Phillis Wheatley, a former slave, became America's first black female poet.

Britain and its colonies. Great Britain tightened its political authority over its American colonies after 1763. The British Parliament passed measures that regulated the American economy, particularly taxation. Americans began to demand freedom from Great Britain. American leaders used expressions of liberty, freedom, and the idea that all men are equal to justify the coming rebellion. The words of the Declaration of Independence, formally separating the colonies from Great Britain, were largely written by thirty-three-year-old Thomas Jefferson, himself a slaveholder. The document mocked the institution of slavery and all slaveholders. The idea that all men are created equal simply cannot be reconciled with the concept of men, women, and children as property.

During the revolutionary years, many slaves gained their freedom by becoming soldiers. At first, there was reluctance to arm slaves to fight against Great Britain, but as the war dragged on, more manpower was needed. Most slaves worked as laborers or served in the navy. A white gentleman who did not wish to fight could pay a black man to substitute for him.

Many slaves simply ran away and joined the English forces. Great Britain took advantage of this and began to recruit actively among the slave population. At the end of the war, four thousand slaves from Savannah, Georgia, six thousand from Charleston, South Carolina, and four thousand from New York ran away, many on English ships.

Slavery in the Young United States

By 1783, the thirteen independent colonies, with the help of French sea and land power, had defeated the British on American soil. Each former colony, now an independent state, developed its own constitution immediately following the end of the war. The new nation was a loose alliance of states, held together by a weak central government with limited powers. Over the years following the revolution, it became clear that a stronger central government was needed to carry out the responsibilities of the new nation.

A constitutional convention met in Philadelphia in 1787 to draw up a new constitution. In addition to creating a new, stronger federal government, the convention showed a new attitude toward slavery that had been developing since the war. One of the first acts of the new United States Congress set up by the Constitution was to pass the Northwest Ordinance. This law forbade slavery north of the Ohio River.

The state governments also passed antislavery laws. By 1789, the gradual abolition (elimination) of slavery had been declared in Pennsylvania. In 1790, there were five state abolitionist organizations, and in Virginia and Maryland, a growing number of people were openly calling for an end to slavery.

Along with new attitudes toward slavery came new status, to an extent, for black people. Free blacks began to occupy positions of importance in New England and the middle colonies. Beginning in 1791, Benjamin Banneker, a black mathematician and astronomer, published a series of almanacs that would become very widely read in postrevolutionary America. Thomas Jefferson, on acknowledging a gift of Banneker's first edition, wrote, "nobody wishes more than I do to see such proofs as you exhibit that nature has given to our black brethren talents equal to those of the other colors of men."[9]

Slavery North and South

Unfortunately, Jefferson's sentiments did not lead him to participate actively in ending slavery in Virginia. The division between the North and the South was heightened by the need for labor in the largely agricultural South. Gradually, the Northern states were abandoning slavery. The commercial interests of the Northern cities and the small, self-sufficient farms of the North could not use slave labor effectively to make a profit.

The South, on the other hand, with its large plantations growing cash crops for sale, such as cotton, rice, and tobacco, could use slavery to its advantage, making enormous profits. Though they had lost many slaves after the American Revolution, the slave states recovered. The invention of the cotton gin in 1793 sealed the question of slavery. This machine, which separated seeds from cotton, made the production of cotton faster and much more profitable. Now there was a need for slaves all year long who could be closely grouped and watched by white overseers. Slaves could be put to work growing and preparing cotton

Thomas Jefferson wrote this letter to black scientist Benjamin Banneker. In it, Jefferson expressed his view that blacks may have talents and abilities equal to those of whites.

The cotton gin, invented by Eli Whitney, made the task of cleaning cotton much faster and easier. By speeding up the process, the machine made cotton more profitable to grow, and increased the South's reliance on slavery.

for market. By 1860, cotton represented 57 percent of America's exports, and employed three quarters of all slave agricultural workers.

Even in those states that were not profiting from cotton, slaves proved useful in different ways. The domestic slave trade was an important source of income for Virginia and the Carolinas by 1820. Rather than using slave labor exclusively themselves, these states exported slaves to the large cotton, sugar, and tobacco plantations of the Deep South. Selling slaves to other farmers often earned Upper South planters more income than their farms could have done. The hiring out of slaves by their owners became big business as well, with about fifty thousand slaves being sent to work for others each year. Sometimes a trusted slave could "hire his own time," paying his master a percentage of his wages toward the purchase of his freedom.[10]

Slave Life

By the mid-1800s, slavery had become firmly entrenched in the South. To justify the institution, proslavery tracts were written. These documents claimed that blacks were biologically inferior, lazy, and showed a lack of responsibility. Some proslavery tracts even claimed that slaves were happy and better off under slavery than they could be free. If Southern slave owners had doubts, they kept them to themselves. Even Northerners visiting a well-managed plantation

Southern slave owners liked to portray their slaves as happy people who enjoyed their lives on the plantation.

run by a kind owner often talked about how contented slaves seemed to be in this "peculiar institution."

Circumstances for slaves varied greatly. Masters ranged from kind to malicious and cruel. Field hands worked hard, growing cotton, indigo, rice, tobacco, and corn as well as other vegetables. Slaves often slept in houses that were made of wooden planks, with dirt floors. Drafts crept through the shacks in cold weather, and the floor became a muddy mess when it rained. Bedding was often no more than a straw mat, and many people were squeezed in a small space, making simple privacy impossible.

The life of a slave could be full of danger and violence. Often, a slave's circumstances depended on the kindness of his or her owner or overseer.

House slaves had better clothes and food and generally an easier workload than field-workers did. They often lived in the houses of their masters. These slaves formed a black aristocracy among other slaves. Slaves in cities had more freedom and recreational outlets than those on plantations, and freed slaves in cities formed their own societies to which select slaves were invited. The biggest fear for slaves of the Upper and

The rights of blacks, slave or free, were severely limited. Laws dictated where and how blacks could live and work. This bill was written to prevent marriages between blacks and whites.

Middle South was being sold down the Mississippi River, especially to the Louisiana sugar plantations, where they would work some sixteen hours at a time in the swampy lands and brutally hot weather.

Free black people in the South had better job opportunities than slaves but few rights. Former slaves needed to carry a certificate of freedom—and in some places had a brand burned into their hands. Without proof of their free status, they could be captured at any moment and sold back into slavery. It was the punishment for breaking even the smallest white-imposed rule. Even in the North, job competition with whites was fierce, and blacks were not allowed to join trade unions. The idea of the inferiority of the black race was no less common among Northerners than it was in the South. However, blacks had more chance for personal and religious expression in the North because slavery was outlawed, and many joined the abolition movement.

Hopes for the End of Slavery

One of the ways proposed to deal with blacks who were freed was colonization. The idea was to free the slaves and send them to live in Africa in a colony of their own. It was popular among those who disliked slavery, but did not want to live as equals with black people. In 1816, the American Colonization Society was founded. Many prominent white citizens were founders and supporters of colonization, and funds were raised from many groups, including the United

States Congress. The society founded the West African colony of Liberia in 1822. However, by this time, many freed slaves had been born in America and did not want to move to a foreign land. They preferred to remain in the United States and work toward an end to racial discrimination.

Other steps were being taken by abolitionists and slaves themselves to help end the peculiar institution.

Even if they did not rebel forcefully, slaves found ways to protest the system that considered them property. Many slaves would deliberately work slowly or break equipment to hurt their owners' interests.

Free blacks and antislavery whites in the North helped runaway slaves escape to freedom on the Underground Railroad. This was a network of people who would pass slaves along from hiding place to hiding place until they reached freedom in the Northern states or Canada, where slavery was illegal. Harriet Tubman, a runaway slave herself, was one of the leaders of this Underground Railroad. She helped many slaves to freedom. Most slaves who attempted escape did so on their own, but only a fortunate few made it as far as the North and freedom. Even those who remained in slavery, however, did what they could to fight the institution. On some plantations, slaves worked slowly or broke equipment to harm their masters' interests in whatever way they could.

As slavery became more entrenched and families were broken up to feed the massive plantations of the Deep South, fugitive slave laws, which returned runaways to their masters, became harsher. Abolitionist words and thought entered the oral slave grapevine, and methods of fighting slavery became fiercer. Slave revolts increased. According to historians Leslie B. Fishel and Benjamin Quarles, "From colonial times to emancipation, there were some 250 slave revolts and conspiracies."[11] The three most significant American slave insurrections were about to occur.

3

WHO WAS NAT TURNER?

It was October 2, 1800. Down in the slave quarters of the small plantation owned by Benjamin Turner in Southampton County, Virginia, the cries of a newborn baby could be heard. Benjamin Turner was a religious man, a devout Methodist. He held prayer services for his slaves and allowed them to go to church on Sunday. The birth of a new baby is usually a joyous occasion. Nat Turner's mother saw it otherwise. According to folktales, Nancy Turner had to be restrained, because she felt she would rather kill her baby than see him grow up in slavery.[1]

Nat's mother had been brought to the United States from her country near the Nile River only five years before Nat was born. She lived through the horrible land marches and then confinement in the lower part of a boat that people destined for New World slavery endured. Barely more than a teenager, she fought her confinement. After she was bought by the Turner family, she "jumped the broomstick." Legal marriage for slaves was outlawed, so those who wished to marry

★ 26 ★

participated in a ritual called "jumping the broomstick." Nancy "married" Nat's father, who was already a slave on the plantation. The name of Nat's father is unknown, but Nat's father's mother was a very religious slave known as Old Bridget. Nat, or Nathaniel, which in Hebrew means "gift of God," was very close to his grandmother. She told him folktales from Africa and stories from the Bible.

A Gifted Child

By the time Nat was three or four years old, his mother, Nancy, had resigned herself to being a slave. She had learned to speak English and probably worked in the house. Nat was a very smart child. It seemed he could learn anything! One day, his mother heard him talking with other children, probably both black and white, because small children played together on the plantations regardless of race or slave status. Nat was talking about something that happened before he was born. When he was asked who had told him about the event, Nat said he just knew. At first, his mother did not believe Nat. Later he said, "I stuck to my story, however, and related some things which went, in her opinion, to confirm it. . . ."[2]

Other people in the slave community were called over to listen to what Nat had to say. They were all amazed and, according to Nat, said, "in my hearing, I surely would be a prophet. . . ." The people gathered noticed that Nat had some bumps on his head and chest. According to African tradition, that meant he would surely become a great leader. Old Bridget had noticed Nat's high intelligence, as had his master. Benjamin Turner said that Nat "had too much sense to be raised, and if I was, I would never be of any service to any one as a slave."[3] Slaves were supposed to be docile and willing—it might cause the master problems if a slave could think for himself.

One day, when he was crying, someone gave Nat a book to look at. Not only did Nat stop crying, but he began to spell out the words attached to the pictures. How had he learned to read? No one, including Nat Turner himself, remembered. But from then on, at every opportunity, he read, particularly the Bible. Though many slave owners discouraged literacy among their slaves, Benjamin Turner seemed proud of Nat and showed him off to guests.

All this attention, and the praise Nat got for being different, formed his personality. If he had been white and the son of the plantation owner, a wonderful, sparkling, successful future would have been predicted for him. But Nat Turner was a slave. There were limits to what this little slave boy could possibly do with this "mind like mine, restless, inquisitive and observant of every thing that was passing."[4]

As Nat Turner grew older, several things happened that made him aware of his lot in life—that of a person owned by other people. To be a slave was to be "property"—and property cannot have a say in its own future. First, Nat's father ran away, as many slaves did. Nothing is known about his relationship with his

A Bill to prevent all persons from teaching
Slaves to read or write, the use of figures
excepted. -

Whereas the teaching of Slaves to read
and write has a tendency to excite dissatisfaction in their minds and to produce insurrections
and rebellion to the manifest injury of the citizens of this State: Therefore

Be it enacted by the General Assembly of
the State of North-Carolina, and it is hereby
enacted by the authority of the same, That a-
ny free person who shall hereafter teach
or attempt to teach any slave within this
State to read or write, the use of figures
excepted, shall be liable to indictment in
any court of record in this State having
jurisdiction thereof; and upon conviction shall at
the discretion of the court if a white man or
woman be fined not less than one hundred dollars
nor more than two hundred dollars or imprisoned
and if a free person of colour shall be whipped at
the discretion of the court not exceeding thirty nine
lashes nor less than twenty lashes

Be it further enacted. That if any slave shall

*Many Southerners, including the authors of this bill,
felt that slaves should not be taught to read or write,
because literacy could lead to rebellion.*

father, but whatever it was, there was one less family member in Nat's little world.

In 1809, Benjamin Turner's son Samuel bought some land from his father. He needed slaves to work in his fields. Benjamin loaned him eight slaves of his own, including Nancy and Nat Turner. When Benjamin died, just a year later, his lands and slaves were divided among his children. Old Bridget also went to live on the Samuel Turner farm with Nat and his mother.

Samuel was even more religious than his father. He carefully selected the Bible passages to be read to his slaves at the prayer meetings. These passages talked about the necessity to obey the master's will absolutely. If they did not, they would surely end up in hell. Being a slave was a black person's lot. It was what God wanted.

How must Nat Turner—a boy of great intelligence, able to read the Bible for himself—have felt about these messages? Perhaps we can interpret from his behavior as he became a young man. He decided to become what everyone had said he was—a very special person. As Nat said later, "Having soon discovered to be great, I must appear so, and therefore studiously avoided mixing in society, and wrapped myself in mystery, devoting my time to fasting and prayer."[5]

By the time Nat was twelve, he was put to work in the cotton, tobacco, and cornfields with the other slaves. His days were endless work, "from can see 'til can't"—that is, from sunup to sundown.[6] The slave diet consisted of cornmeal mush, bacon fat, and, occasionally, some vegetables grown by the slaves themselves in a small plot near their cabin. Nat picked cotton, sowed corn and tobacco, milked cows, hoed fields, harvested tobacco and corn, and did the many repair chores required to maintain a large farm. All of a sudden there was no more play with the white children—they were now his masters. If he were tired, he could never choose to sit down. Any time of his own had to be wedged in after the endless work.

All this time, Nat continued to read whatever he could. He managed to get looks at the schoolbooks the

Nat Turner worked at growing and processing tobacco on his owners' plantations, as these slaves are doing.

white children brought home. He later said; "all my time, not devoted to my master's service, was spent either in prayer, or in making experiments in casting different things in molds made of earth. . . ."[7] He absolutely refused to steal anything. The other slaves admired him and believed that his knowledge and self-discipline came directly from God.

Nat Turner, Prophet

As Nat grew up, more and more slave churches were being led by free black preachers. Most slave masters believed that Christianity would help "civilize" their slaves, and that hearing the message from members of their own race would make it stick. Nat went to these meetings and took in a Christian message that was very different from the one Samuel Turner wanted his slaves to learn. Using African myths and Christian beliefs, the black preachers told the slaves that slavery was evil, and that there would come a time when the sad life and the beatings they endured would be over. Preachers gave slaves hope and allowed them to vent their feelings. Though still a slave, Nat Turner, already respected by fellow slaves for his reading ability, began preaching. Little by little, he became a recognized preacher at whatever forest hideout or abandoned shack the slaves could manage to meet in for prayer meetings.

Nat Turner began to claim he was having revelations, saying later that he had heard voices in the wind, explaining biblical passages. He believed this was God speaking to him, and that he was meant for some special purpose. After a cruel overseer, a man hired to supervise the slaves, arrived at the Turner plantation, Nat ran away, as his father had done. Thirty days after he had left, however, Nat Turner came back on his own. Many other runaway slaves returned to their masters voluntarily. Very few actually escaped to freedom. Though many slaves came back to their masters, few—if any—had Turner's abilities. Some of the other slaves looked down on Turner for returning. Turner claimed later that God had told him that he must fulfill his destiny, which was yet to be revealed.[8] Turner was to return to his master because the great purpose he was supposed to fulfill was to be found with his fellow slaves.

Marriage and Family

After Nat Turner's return to slavery, he married a slave named Cherry and continued to work in the fields, think, and pray. In 1822, Samuel Turner, only ten years older than twenty-two-year-old Nat, died. What would happen to the slaves now? Samuel's children were still too young to take over the farm. All except three house slaves, including Nat Turner's mother, would be sold. The worst fear to slaves in the Upper South states like Virginia was to be "sold down the Mississippi," to one of the plantations of the Deep South. These plantations were larger and used slaves even more like expendable animals than the farms of Virginia and the Carolinas did. Rumor along the slave grapevine was that slaves were treated like cattle at these huge plantations, and families were never kept together. The weather was also brutal and caused many slaves to become ill or die.

Though Nat Turner and Cherry were sold to different plantations, they both remained in Southampton County. The worst had not been realized. Still, they saw each other only seldom. Turner could not watch his three children grow up or be there to protect them.

Nat Turner now had a new owner. Thomas Moore bought Turner at an auction for four hundred dollars to do heavy work around Moore's farm. Turner had known Sally Francis Moore, Thomas's wife, since childhood. He had even played with her brother when they were both little. Though the Moores were not harsh with their few slaves, there was much work to be done around the growing farm. The work went on constantly, day in and day out, from sunrise to dark.

Visions of the Prophet

It was about this time that Nat Turner claimed he began having visions. More and more he had kept to himself, using his little free time from work to fast and pray. He read the Bible and searched for ways to solve the mystery of his visions. Some of his visions involved white spirits and black spirits fighting with each other. He heard voices telling him that God had spoken, that Turner was indeed a prophet, and that he must become a minister to his people. Nat Turner quickly became one of the favorite and most influential slave preachers. Slaves came to hear about the visions Turner had seen, such as drops of blood on corn. He had also seen letters, numbers, and figures of men on leaves in the woods. Some of the human figures were doing battle.[9]

To the slaves, whose daily lives left no hope for a better one, Nat Turner's sermons were enjoyed as wonderful dramatic events. Though Turner was never an ordained preacher, he was recognized by the slave community as a prophet. He even claimed to have cured one ill slave and said he had the power to heal others.

Most of the white people to whom Turner spoke about his visions laughed at him. They thought he must be harmless. It did not seem at all dangerous to let him gabble away to other slaves on Sundays. He was, after all, a good worker and very honest. A few whites, however, thought Turner had gone too far. They feared he might stir up trouble among the other slaves. But they were in the minority, and Nat Turner continued to preach.

Turner traveled around the countryside on Sundays as his popularity increased. He knew all the plantations and farms in the area, and how to get around on the winding country lanes and roads. He also met a few free blacks whose lives were still very hard. Though they had freedom, they had very few rights, and they could not vote. Often, their wives were still in slavery.

One of the events that occurred during those preaching years was the baptism of a white overseer. Etheldred T. Brantley believed that Turner had healed him of an unknown illness and purged him of various demons. No white church would allow this black slave to baptize a white man, so Turner took Brantley to a

Nat Turner became widely respected as a preacher and, according to many of his fellow slaves, a prophet.

millpond in the deep forest. A crowd of both white and black people gathered. Turner later said, "we went down to the water together, in the sight of many who reviled us, and were baptized by the Spirit—After this I rejoiced greatly, and gave thanks to God."[10]

A Violent Vision

The more he traveled and the more he preached, the more Turner felt he had a mission. He came to know about twenty men, slave and free, whom he felt he could trust to help him carry out his plans. On May 12, 1828, Nat Turner had a vision that would influence the course of American history. He said he heard a loud noise above him. Then a voice told him that he should take on the burden of Christ and fight against evil, which was loose in the land: "for the time was fast approaching when the first should be last and the last should be first. . . . I should arise and prepare myself, and slay my enemies with their own weapons."[11]

Turner vowed silence until he saw a sign that would tell him to begin the work of making slaves their own masters. However, he did something that could have destroyed his plan entirely if he had been taken seriously. Turner told his master, Thomas Moore, "the slaves ought to be free and would be 'one day or other.' Shocked at such rebellious talk from a slave, Moore took Turner to the shed and gave him a thrashing."[12] Turner continued to work as a slave by day, and preached and planned at night and on Sundays. All the while, though, he waited for a sign.

4

LEADING UP TO NAT TURNER

On the French-held island of Santo Domingo, located in the West Indies, south and east of Florida, there were many free blacks who could read and write. Their desire to free all blacks from the oppression of slavery and their ability to organize led, in 1790, to a long and brutal insurrection. Although the white French population and many soldiers resisted, the insurgents were victorious. They established the first black republic— Haiti—in the New World. The cost of this independence was some sixty thousand lives, both black and white.

News of this successful rebellion reached the American South, and the period between 1790 and 1831 was one of extreme discomfort for slave owners. Particularly in Virginia and the Carolinas, where small revolts by slaves occurred frequently, this was a time of anxiety. Even in the backcountry of Southampton County, Virginia, there had been an incident. White slave drivers were bringing a wagonload of slaves from Maryland through Southampton County to be sold in

Toussaint L'Ouverture was the leader of the slaves who successfully rebelled in Santo Domingo, creating the free black republic of Haiti.

Georgia. Several of the desperate slaves tried to escape. In the process, two whites were killed. The frightened Virginians called it a slave revolt, and four of the slaves were hanged. There was even a rumor that slaves who rebelled against their masters were infected with an illness called the Santo Domingo virus. This "infection" could make otherwise docile American slaves delirious, causing them to run away and commit murder![1]

Gabriel Prosser's Slave Revolt

It is clear that any answer other than the obvious one—that slavery itself was an inhuman, intolerable institution that had to end—was sought to end the problems facing slave owners. Even ridiculous answers were better than facing reality. But the insurrections would not go away.

In 1800, the year Nat Turner was born, a literate slave and skilled blacksmith named Gabriel Prosser was plotting to capture the city of Richmond, Virginia. The conspiracy was formed by Prosser and other skilled slaves living in Richmond. These slaves had read the Declaration of Independence. They knew it said that all men were created equal. And, as had happened in the American and French revolutions when people wanted to be free of rules that were unfair, they believed they had the right to rebel against those who were holding them in bondage.

The leaders of the Prosser conspiracy went into black churches and spoke about the evils of slavery. They talked to plantation slaves about its unfairness.

The plan was to fight only those who believed in slavery. They would spare others, such as Quakers, who opposed the institution. Prosser wanted to make a silk flag that said, "Death or Liberty." He would carry it into a battle that would burn Richmond and take the governor, James Monroe, as a hostage.

Unfortunately, the plantation slaves never fully supported Prosser's plans. Betrayed by informers and foiled by bad weather, Gabriel Prosser and thirty-four fellow rebels were arrested by the state militia before one shot was fired. Believing that they were right and that other people would perhaps carry on their work, the rebels made a vow of silence about their thwarted plans. Prosser and all the rebels were hanged, displaying great courage and total silence until the end.

Virginians were shocked and terrified, and they began to fear slave rebellions hatching everywhere. The fact that the conspirators were so brave and so willing to die for their beliefs, if necessary, was doubly frightening. Any debate about ending slavery was conducted behind closed doors. The result was more militia and stronger enforcement of slave codes—laws that defined what slaves could and could not do. Much talk about colonizing—sending free blacks away to some other state or country—went on, with no result. The one good thing that happened in Virginia as a direct result of the Prosser conspiracy was the ending of international slave trade in that state. Even this, however, was not undertaken for humanitarian reasons. It was done so that native Africans, who had not been properly subdued, would no longer be brought to the state.

Virginia was worried about its slave population, which in many counties resulted in blacks outnumbering whites, but it also had other concerns. During the 1820s, a drought and a general depletion of soil on overused land caused crop failure and financial depression. Although slave owners in Virginia prided themselves on being kind to their slaves, financial failure often meant they could afford fewer slaves to do more of the work. The threat of being sold South grew for the slaves at the same time that their few freedoms were being limited due to fear of revolt.

Denmark Vesey Plans a Rebellion

Denmark Vesey was a literate carpenter who had bought his freedom. He traveled and read a great deal, especially published accounts of congressional debates that challenged slavery at its roots. Vesey, like Gabriel Prosser, believed in the Declaration of Independence. It made him furious that white men interpreted it to exclude blacks. Some of his children were still in slavery, and he was powerless to help them. He lectured to many groups and gathered followers.

Vesey and his followers planned a surprise attack on Charleston, South Carolina. A lookout was to give a signal, at midnight, that all was well. Then, six battle units would go into different parts of the city and capture it. What they would do after that was unclear. The plotters never found out. As had happened in the

Prosser conspiracy, Vesey and his followers were betrayed by loyal house slaves, who told their white masters about the plot. The military overran the Charleston slums, where the rebellion's leaders lived. No shot was fired. Again, thirty-four men, plus Denmark Vesey, went to their deaths by hanging. Thirty-seven other blacks were transported from the state.

In the aftermath of this failed insurrection, South Carolina passed a law that allowed black sailors arriving in Charleston to be imprisoned, because they might have been to Haiti, where the successful slave insurrection took place. Vigilante committees were formed throughout the Carolinas and Virginia. In Charleston, devastating fires, which broke out almost nightly from Christmas Eve, 1825, through early summer, were blamed on slaves.[2] Any black person who seemed remotely guilty was convicted of arson. Other small conspiracies flared up momentarily and were extinguished. The Southerners reacted, as usual, by tightening slave codes and increasing the military presence. Virginia became an armed camp.

Growth of the Abolition Movement

Many in the South blamed the abolitionists for the insurrection plots. Someone had to be blamed. To admit that slaves could think for themselves would call into question the idea that Southerners were enslaving a less-than-human race. Free blacks in the Northern cities, who were able to speak out and join abolitionist organizations, and Southern slaves, whose dissatisfaction was stimulated by Northern visitors and preachers who could read, combined to make the climate of the South increasingly uncomfortable for slave owners.

As the 1820s ended and the 1830s began, anti-slavery sentiment in the North was growing. The first all-black newspaper, *Freedom's Journal*, was up and running. A free black named David Walker published an abolitionist tract called *Appeal to the Colored Citizens of the World* in Boston in 1829. He encouraged, even raged, at blacks to stand up for themselves.[3]

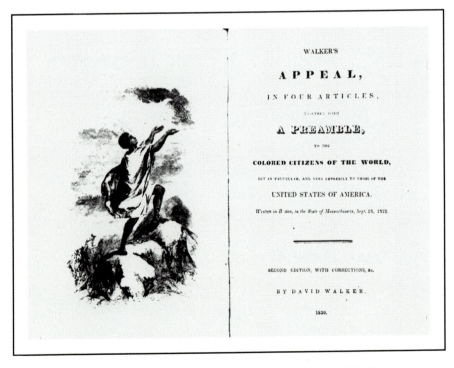

David Walker published his Appeal, *encouraging blacks to stand up for themselves and to resist slavery, in 1829.*

EXECUTIVE DEPARTMENT,

Raleigh, August 19, 1830.

Sir,

I received a few days since from the Magistrate of Police for the town of Wilmington, a communication, stating that a well disposed free person of color had put into the hands of the Commissioners for that town, a pamphlet, published by one *David Walker*, of Boston; treating in most inflamatory terms of the condition of the slaves in the southern States—exaggerating their sufferings—magnifying their physical strength, and underrating the power of the whites—containing also an open appeal to their natural love of liberty; and expressing throughout, sentiments totally subversive of all subordination in our slaves. An investigation of the affair has shown, that the author had an agent in that place, *a slave*, who had received the books, with instructions to distribute them throughout the State, and particularly in Newbern, Fayetteville and Elizabeth. It is impossible to ascertain from this agent, to what extent they have been distributed; but the fellow is now in jail, and every effort is making to develope the whole transaction in its fullest extent; and they have been so far developed, as to prove, that a very general and extensive impression has been made on the minds of the negroes in the vicinity of Wilmington, that measures had been taken towards their emancipation at a certain, and not very distant day; and, moreover, that a certain number of free persons of color, and a few slaves, have for months past, frequently discussed the subject of a conspiracy, to effect the emancipation of the slaves in that portion of the State. How far this project has extended, it is impossible to say; but every means which the existing laws of the State place within the reach of its citizens, should be promptly used, and more particularly by the Police officers of the towns on the seaboard, to ascertain the extent of the mischief contemplated, and particularly to prevent the dissemmination of Walker's pamphlet—the mischievous tendency of which is obvious to every one, and the design of which cannot be mistaken.

The circulation of this book having been noticed in Louisianna, Georgia, South Carolina and Virginia; and more recently discovered in our own State, proves beyond a doubt, that a systematic attempt is making by some reckless persons at the North, to sow sedition among the slaves of the South; and that this pamphlet is intended, and well calculated to prepare the minds of the slave population for any measure, however desperate.

It is mortifying to know, that we are suffering an evil, without the possibility of a remedy, and that we live under a government where such an offence may be perpetrated with impunity.

We have no remedy against the wretch, whose book is scattered abroad throughout our land, and a very inadequate one against the poor deluded slave, who may permit himself to become his agent.

I beg you will lay this matter before the police of your town, and invite their prompt attention to the necessity of arresting the circulation of the book alluded to; and I would suggest the necessity of the most vigilant execution of your police laws, and the laws of the State; and if, in the course of the investigation, any thing should transpire by which it may reasonably be believed that an agent, or agents, have been employed in your neighborhood, I should be glad to have this Department informed of it, with as little delay as possible.

I have the honor to be

Your obedient servant.

Gio. Owen

Nathaniel Bruce Esquire

One of the Commissioners of the Town of Edenton

Walker's Appeal *terrified and enraged white slave owners all over the South. In some places, efforts were made, including this circular urging the confiscation of* Walker's Appeal, *to keep such abolitionist literature out of the hands of black slaves.*

In 1831, a copy of Walker's tract was found in the house of a literate free black man. Virginians were alarmed. Laws were passed to prohibit public teaching to both free blacks and slaves.

William Lloyd Garrison, a long-time abolitionist, published *The Liberator*, a newspaper demanding total emancipation, immediately. His first issue came out on January 1, 1831. Garrison predicted violence to come if slavery were not abolished soon.[4] Perhaps Nat Turner, the too-smart slave boy who had learned to read and write at an early age, read at least parts of these antislavery publications.

N at Turner's belief that he was called by God for a special purpose was formed long before the abolitionist tracts began to filter into Virginia. However, by the time Turner had his final visions, and came to believe that his purpose was to correct the imbalance between blacks and

THE STAGE IS SET

whites, those tracts were around. It is difficult to believe that Nat Turner did not know that other slaves had revolted before him. He believed himself to be a prophet. If he heard other people speak of equality and the right to rebellion through the slave grapevine, it could only have solidified this purpose. We do not know that for certain, because he never said so. We really only know what was written down, by a white man, in the confessions that Nat Turner made in jail. Aside from these confessions, there is very little information about what went on as Turner planned for what came to be called the Nat Turner Rebellion, or the Southampton Insurrection.

Waiting for a Sign

According to the confessions, Turner had experienced a vision in which God seemed to speak to him, telling him, "I should arise and prepare myself, and slay my enemies with their own weapons."[1] So, he waited for the sign that would tell him when to begin. It did not come as fast as he would have hoped, and while he waited, he became the property of yet another master. Thomas Moore died in 1828, and all his property went to his nine-year-old son, Putnam. Women had few rights in 1828, and when Putnam's mother, Sally Moore, married Joseph Travis in 1829, Travis controlled his own and Putnam's slaves.

Despite the fact that Nat Turner was recognized by slaves and slave owners in Southampton County as a smart and special slave preacher with obvious skill, he never became a house slave. Perhaps the very fact that he was so intelligent and literate made it necessary for his owners to keep him in the field. As long as Nat hoed the fields and kept quiet, his masters appeared willing to tolerate his preaching.

Everything changed in February 1831. Throughout history, the unusual phenomenon of a solar eclipse has brought about fears of the end of the world, and hopes that a new order would arise. Southampton County, Virginia, noticed this event. For Nat Turner, waiting impatiently for a sign that God would lead him to the next step in his mission, the eclipse of the sun on February 12 was all he needed.[2]

God had spoken to him, and he called in his troops. Four slaves he felt he could trust were told what God had called him to do. They were to go out among other slaves and find others who would join an insurrection. The four "generals," all trusted slaves on their plantations, took in Nat Turner's elaborate religious papers detailing his findings and maps of how to proceed. A plan of action and various people to involve began to take shape.

The Plot Begins to Form

The original idea was to begin the rebellion on July 4—Independence Day. But no one could agree on actual plans. Then Nat Turner became ill and was not able to coordinate the insurrection on July 4. In fact, Turner admitted later that, despite his convictions about the evils of slavery, it was very difficult to begin a rebellion that would mean the deaths of so many people he had known all his life.[3]

Again, a natural phenomenon urged the rebellion ahead. An unexplained atmospheric change disturbed the light of the sun on Saturday, August 13. The sun's light grew faint, and then changed colors, from green to blue to white. Even the air became moist and heavy. Many believed this to be a sign of coming evil, especially when a dark spot could be seen on the sun. Occasionally, due to atmospheric disturbance, these dark depressions—cooler parts of the sun—can be seen by human eyes. Scientists of the time already knew what caused these sunspots, but most ordinary people did not. So, when the spot could be seen on the sun, all kinds of fanciful interpretations surfaced. For Nat Turner, the sunspot was a sign to begin his insurrection.

He told his trusted four "as the black spot has passed over the sun, so would the blacks pass over the earth."[4]

During the week following the sunspot phenomenon, rumors flew. Church services seemed unsettled. Slaves said things to their masters that they would have been afraid to say before. Slaves were talking among themselves. Something was going on. Would the slaves rise against their oppressors? How safe would that be? Was there someone who could lead them out of slavery? Or was it safer to just stay put?

Sunday morning, August 21, was a typical hot, humid summer day. White families rode off to church, and slaves were left home for a day of rest. Most Southampton County slave owners were really just small farmers who worked alongside their slaves. Joseph Travis, Nat Turner's current owner, believed he had no reason to worry about leaving a trusted slave alone for the entire day.[5]

The Conspirators

In the thick forests around the farms and plantations, slaves had established special meeting places where they could enjoy getting together in their scant free time. One of these places was called Cabin Pond. It was there that Nat Turner planned to meet with his trusted fellow conspirators, and there others would join them. Early arrivals roasted a pig and drank apple brandy. By the time Nat Turner arrived, his trusted four—Hark, Nelson, Henry, and Sam—were waiting for instructions, along with slaves named Jack and Will

Nat Turner met with his fellow insurrection leaders in a place called Cabin Pond. He is seen here, urging them to join the rebellion.

Francis. Turner questioned Will Francis, whom he did not know. When Will said that he would either win his freedom or die trying, Turner admitted him to the inner circle.[6]

The plan was to strike that very night. Sunday was a quiet time for families who had been out visiting during the day. Slave owners were used to hearing blacks out in the woods in August, hunting, before the work week began. August was the month referred to as "jubilee." This was the time when most of the crops were doing well by themselves, and the busy season of harvesting had not yet begun. The whites would never expect what was about to happen, and would be so frightened that it all would be over soon.

Nat Turner knew that, when many people were told about plans for insurrection, betrayal became more likely. Rather than telling too many about his plans, he wanted to attack by surprise, gathering slave recruits from the farms as each white family was killed. Nat Turner quoted from the biblical prophet Ezekiel, saying that all must be killed, even the children.

Turner believed that the spreading rumors and the grumbling that had been going on all summer would guarantee that other slaves would join the rebellion. Then, the expanded army would go into the county seat, called Jerusalem, where they would declare victory over all of Southampton County.

It is not clear what Nat Turner planned to do after his army had taken Jerusalem. Perhaps he hoped to establish a black stronghold in the Dismal Swamp, a wretched, difficult place where runaway slaves had been hiding for decades. Because Turner believed he was God's prophet, perhaps he thought God would give him a sign about what to do next after the death and destruction was over. The first objective was to kill every white person—young or old, woman or man— on the path to Jerusalem. The first farm they passed was to be spared. It belonged to Giles Reese, where Turner's wife, Cherry, and children lived. Cherry had Turner's sacred papers with the drawings and odd lettering, and a paper that contained the names of the conspirators.

Midnight arrived. It was now Monday, August 22. A torch was lit and the seven rebels made their way through the woods to the Joseph Travis farm. Extinguishing the torch, they drew their axes and crept though the dark night toward the house.

THE
SOUTHAMPTON
INSURRECTION

Nat Turner climbed a ladder to the second-story window, then went downstairs and opened the front door to admit his little army. Entering the bedroom of Joseph and Sally Travis, the men waited for Nat Turner to lift his hatchet and become the first to take the life of a white man, this one his master.

Turner swung wildly, just grazing Travis's head. Will, who would prove to be the most vicious of all the insurgents, used his ax to kill both Sally and Joseph Travis. Also in the house that fateful dawn were Putnam Moore—the eleven-year-old boy who had become Nat Turner's legal owner when Thomas Moore died, and Joel Westbrook—a fourteen-year-old boy who was an apprentice in Joseph Travis's wheelwright shop. They, too, fell to the avenging army.

When all the whites in the house were killed, Turner and his lieutenants moved on to the next farm. They gathered any firearms they could find, practiced military drills, and went on to farm after farm, killing every white person they could find. Not all of the slaves on the farms welcomed them. Some even hid their masters and mistresses from the violent rebels. Many slaves ran off into the woods, terrified. A few other slaves joined the band, more from not knowing what else to do than because of conviction.

As daylight came, Nat Turner himself had killed no one. Finally, one young girl, Margaret Whitehead, who had almost escaped by hiding between two chimneys, was spotted by Turner. He chased her into a field and killed her with his sword and an old fence post.[1] Her sister, Harriet, was saved by a family slave, but then ran off into the forest in fear that this slave, too, would take part in the killing.

The Panic Spreads

The few white people who escaped began running from farm to farm. Word spread about the unspeakable violence and death awaiting all the whites in the area. Loyal slaves who had witnessed the killings at the first two farms spread the word to other slaves, who warned their masters. Farms were deserted as slave owners ran into the woods or headed for Jerusalem. Panic and hysteria were everywhere.

Horses had been taken at the massacre sites, and Will now commanded a cavalry unit. Nat Turner took his infantry in another direction. The rebels now numbered about seventeen in all. They knew that word had spread and that the local militia would soon be coming after them. Many farms were, by now, already deserted, but the killing continued at any place that still held white people. Nat Turner rode after the two columns,

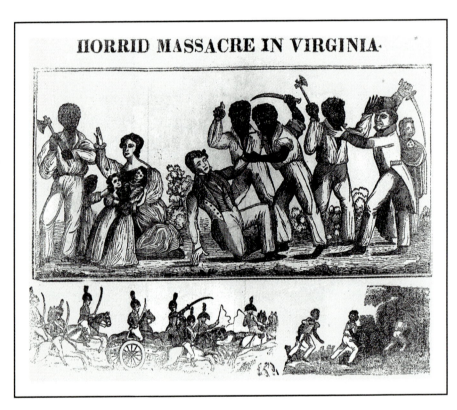

Southerners reacted to news of the Turner Rebellion with shock and horror.

which now were several because some of the new recruits had become separated from the original infantry unit. Finally, all the rebel forces met at a deserted plantation. By this time, Turner's army numbered forty, though some recruits were still reluctant.

One man, a black overseer named Aaron Harris, told the assembled blacks that they should not continue with the bloody revolt. This was no longer a surprise attack. There were too many whites with too many soldiers and guns, and they would all be here soon. Escape now, Harris urged.[2]

Nat Turner disagreed. If only enough slaves joined them, they would be victorious. They must continue to march to Jerusalem. They set out, riding fast into the yards of any homestead where people had not yet fled. Unfortunately, many of the slave soldiers had raided the brandy cellars of the slaughtered families, and the bulk of their army was meandering rather than marching. Nat Turner himself kept to the rear.

Rumors and Reaction

Rumors flew among the people of the county. One rumor claimed that the British had invaded the county and were killing people. Some slaves believed it was high time that white people were being punished for the way they had treated black people for centuries. The major emotion among the slaves, however, was fear—fear of what was going to happen to them when the white militia figured out what was happening. As Aaron Harris had said, there were many white people, many more than in heavily black Southampton County. And there would be a great cry for revenge.

The white population also heard the rumor that the British had invaded and the country was at war with England. But by midmorning on August 22, it was clear that a slave revolt, not a British invasion, was taking place. This time, the surprise attack hoped for by Gabriel Prosser and Denmark Vesey actually had been a surprise. It was rumored that the slave army was reaching a thousand. Church bells tolled and whole families hurtled into Jerusalem. Farmers who went to join the militia locked their wives and children inside any building that seemed strong enough to withstand an attack.

One of the most horrifying spectacles of the whole bloody insurrection took place at a schoolhouse, where ten children were attacked and killed. The schoolhouse was near the farm of a man named Levi Waller, who was in his orchard and watched helplessly as his wife and two daughters were murdered. He was the first white person to escape who had actually seen Nat Turner. Waller reported that Nat Turner rode up after the killing was done. Though Nat Turner was only about five feet seven inches tall and weighed no more than one hundred fifty pounds, he had broad shoulders and large, deep-set eyes. He was carrying a silver sword and he was clearly in charge.[3] His slave soldiers were standing in the yard, drinking, and Turner broke up their party. One of the rebels, Sam Edwards, was having a hard time with the killing. Edwards was crying.

Turner ordered him to get on his horse. He waited until the cavalry, especially the new recruits who were showing the effects of the brandy, were riding. Then Nat Turner led them out of the gate and once again formed the rebels into a rear column.

Chasing the Rebels

Two groups of armed white men were on the trail of the insurgents by noon. One of the armed groups came upon the schoolhouse less than half an hour after the rebels had left. All they found of the rebel force was one of Levi Waller's slaves, Albert, drunk in the middle of the road. The punishment of the rebels started there. The first citizens' militia unit crippled Albert, and when a military unit came by later in the afternoon, its members killed him.

Though several other homesteads fell to the fury of the slave rebels, most homesteads were by now deserted. Nat Turner himself did no more of the killing, though it is unknown why that was so. In addition to sparing the home of Giles Reese, Turner had ordered several other homesteads to be left alone. These included the homes of poor whites who owned no slaves, and the Turner farm, the place where Nat Turner was born and had spent his boyhood.

Though the slave army now numbered close to seventy, some of the slaves had already deserted, and many of the other rebels were too drunk to fight. The plan now was to march into Jerusalem and capture arms and ammunition. The march was interrupted by yet

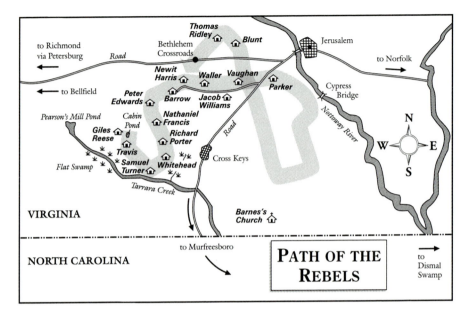

Turner and his rebels weaved a path through Southampton County, stopping to kill any white person they could find.

another drinking bout, then an inevitable meeting with a small detachment of armed white men.

A Battle Occurs

The only actual armed conflict of this short but brutal war then occurred. The white captain's horse bolted at the sound of a musket, and he was thrown into the line of armed black rebels.[4] Noise and confusion reigned as horses stampeded and carried men everywhere but where they wanted to be. The slaves persisted, and many of the white volunteers retreated. Encouraged by this, the slaves kept chasing the whites.[5] More white volunteers arrived. This time, they drove the rebels back.

The white volunteers' guns worked better than those that had been confiscated by the rebels, and six rebels were shot. Some of the drunk rebels headed for home, and one of the wounded men, Dred Francis, escaped.

The rebel army headed for the forest, with Turner in charge of his retreating men. He planned to go into Jerusalem on a back road and again gain the advantage of a surprise attack.[6] As Turner's dwindling army made its way out of the forest, they found armed white men everywhere. Nat Turner ordered all drinking to stop at once. Alcohol was more the enemy of the rebels than the white men. The rebel troops headed south, finding no more homesteads with people on them. At the Ridley plantation, where Turner hoped to recruit more slaves, they found instead militia and barricades. The rebels spent the night in the woods.

The remaining rebel troops, now sober, were reinforced by new recruits from several large plantations. Turner hoped that still more slaves would join the forty men he had with him. He had not given up. It was Monday night, and sentinels were posted while Turner and the exhausted rebels tried to sleep.

The Rebellion Falls Apart

By Tuesday morning, when a guard woke everyone with word that the white militia was attacking, all the new recruits had panicked and deserted. Only twenty men were left. The rebels needed more men if they were to attack Jerusalem. There were sixty slaves on Dr. Simon Blunt's nearby plantation. Though the place seemed to be deserted, Turner and his men thought there might be slaves in the cabins. As the group neared the house, guns exploded. Several white men blasted away at the rebels from close range. Hark was injured. The horses stampeded. Worst of all, the plantation slaves attacked the group, capturing several rebels.

Nat Turner tried to find his scattered army, only to encounter another group of armed white men. A ferocious, short battle raged in the woods. Three more rebels were shot and killed. Nat Turner and four others escaped through the woods. Still in command, and refusing to let go of his dream of a successful insurrection, Nat Turner sent two of the men, Curtis and Stephen Ridley, to recruit new volunteers. John Clark Turner, spared by Nat Turner on the bloody trail through the homesteads, arrested the Ridleys at gunpoint and herded them to the little village of Cross Keys, where the jail was already full of rebels.

Nat Turner, another slave named Nat, and a slave named Jacob hid in the woods near the Travis farm. Sending Nat and Jacob to try to find other insurgents, Nat Turner waited for them near Cabin Pond, where just two nights before, he had planned the rebellion that seemed now to be falling apart.

SWIFT REPRISAL

It was not until Thursday, August 25, that any organized resistance to the rebellion really began. Before that, rumors, refugees, militias, and federal troops simply made the confusion in Jerusalem worse. The worst rumors said that the slave rebellion was being carried out by an organized army, more than one thousand strong, and that other rebellions were going on all over Virginia and North Carolina.

Newspapers Report the Rebellion

The editor of the *Whig*, a Richmond, Virginia, newspaper, arrived in Jerusalem on August 25 and sent reports back to his paper. In that time, before computers, telephones, or even telegraphs, all news had to be sent by mail or messenger. John Hampden Pleasants, the editor, did not have his first story printed in the paper until August 29. He told about the crowding in Jerusalem, and he also said that the numbers of slaves involved in the insurrection had been exaggerated greatly. By then, he did know about specific families who had been attacked and killed by the rebels, and he included their names in his report. He also knew that the number of slaves involved in the rebellion was somewhere between forty and one hundred:

> Twelve armed and resolute men, were certainly competent to have quelled them at any time. But, taken by surprise—with such horrors before their eyes, and trembling for their wives and children, the men, most naturally, only thought in the first place, of providing a refuge for those dependent upon them. Since this has been effected, the citizens have acted with vigor. Various parties have scoured the country, and a number of the insurgents . . . have been killed or taken. . . . The Preacher-Captain [Nat Turner] has not been taken. . . . The people are naturally enough, wound up to a high pitch of rage, and precaution is even necessary, to protect the lives of the captives . . . the insurrection may be considered as already suppressed.[1]

Putting Down the Rebellion

The reprisals continued. By Tuesday, while Nat Turner hid near Cabin Pond, wondering what had happened to his army, a virtual "massacre of the blacks of Southampton began," wrote historian Eric Foner.[2] Blacks, both free and slave, were being tortured and killed. Militia units rode hard through the backcountry, killing any black person they found in their path. Though the Southampton Insurrection had claimed the lives of sixty whites, the revenge killings by whites brought the death toll into the hundreds.[3]

Finally, one of the militia commanders, General Richard Eppes, sent home many of the military units

SOURCE DOCUMENT

SO MUCH CURIOSITY HAS BEEN EXCITED IN THE STATE, AND SO MUCH EXAGGERATION WILL GO ABROAD, THAT WE HAVE DETERMINED TO DEVOTE A GREAT PORTION OF THIS DAY'S PAPER TO THE STRANGE EVENTS IN THE COUNTY OF SOUTHAMPTON. . . . WHAT STRIKES US AS THE MOST REMARKABLE THING IN THIS MATTER IS THE HORRIBLE FEROCITY OF THESE MONSTERS. THEY REMIND ONE OF A PARCEL OF BLOOD-THIRSTY WOLVES. . . . [N]EITHER AGE NOR SEX IS RESPECTED—THE HELPLESSNESS OF WOMEN AND CHILDREN PLEADS IN VAIN FOR MERCY. THE DANGER IS THOUGHT TO BE OVER—BUT PRUDENCE STILL DEMANDS PRECAUTION. THE LOWER COUNTRY SHOULD BE ON ALERT.— THE CASE OF NAT TURNER WARNS US. NO BLACK MAN OUGHT TO BE PERMITTED TO TURN A PREACHER THROUGH THE COUNTRY. THE LAW MUST BE ENFORCED OR THE TRAGEDY OF SOUTHAMPTON APPEALS TO US IN VAIN.[4]

This report from the Richmond Enquirer *demonstrates the South's initial reaction to the Southampton Insurrection. The article shows that Southerners were afraid and were prepared to urge stronger measures to keep black slaves under control.*

that had arrived in Jerusalem to quell what had been thought to be a huge slave rebellion. Pleasants wrote in his report to the Richmond *Whig*, "To the great honor of General Eppes, he used every precaution in his power . . . to put a stop to the disgraceful procedure" of inflicting revenge on all blacks. "Let the fact not be doubted by those whom it most concerns, that another such insurrection will be the signal for the extirpation of the whole black population in the quarter of the State where it occurs. . . ."[5]

Nat Turner Is Identified

Eyewitness reports from whites who had escaped death but who had seen the rebels, identified Nat Turner as the insurrection's leader. This was surprising to people who had known Nat Turner as a smart, peaceful slave, who was called a preacher by other slaves. Turner had been considered harmless—a small man, working in the fields.

A report to the Richmond *Whig* said that "Nat in person, is not remarkable, his nose is flat, his stature rather small, and hair very thin, without any peculiarity of expression."[6]

And just where was this "not remarkable" slave who had led the only successful surprise slave rebellion in United States history? "The universal opinion in that part of the country, is that Nat, a slave, a preacher and a pretended prophet, was the first contriver, the actual leader. . . ." In John Hampden Pleasants's first dispatches back to Richmond, he speculated about this elusive leader, not seen since "the skirmish in Parker's cornfield, which was in fact, the termination of the insurrection. . . ." White slave owners who had known Turner as well as captured rebels had spoken about him and about his visions. Pleasants concluded that Turner was literate and, as a preacher, had great influence over the Southampton slave population. He also believed that Turner was a religious fanatic who believed that God would lead his troops to victory but who had no practical plan for that victory.[7]

At some time after the end of the insurrection, while authorities were searching for Nat Turner, Turner's papers with drawings of his visions were read by someone who wrote a lengthy letter to the Richmond *Whig*. Because this letter was unsigned, historians have speculated about its authorship, though all have agreed that it was one of the court-appointed lawyers for the slave rebels. It was probably Thomas R. Gray, the man responsible for writing down Nat Turner's confessions, who said, ". . . I have in my possession, some papers given up by his wife, under the lash—they are filled with hieroglyphical characters, conveying no definite meaning."[8] In other words, Turner's wife, Cherry, with whom he left his papers for safekeeping, was whipped to force her to give them up.

Rumors flew about Turner's whereabouts. Perhaps he had fled the state and was preaching elsewhere, inciting more slaves to revolution. Maybe he was deep in the Dismal Swamp, gathering another army. Or maybe he was just hiding out in somebody's slave quarters, helped by other slaves.

Panic in the South

All over the South, slave owners saw insurrection behind every haystack, treachery in kitchen conversations. Rumors continued to fly. Charleston, South

Carolina, reeling from the recent fires, formed a new special cavalry to guard the city.

The people of the counties in North Carolina that formed the border with Virginia were in a state of panic. Refugees gathered in the towns and mingled with the armed and confused militia. All black preachers were suspected of stirring up the slave population. Rumor spread that the Southampton Insurrection was merely part of a larger rebellion, and the North Carolina militia awaited orders. Maybe Nat Turner himself, still at large, was going to lead this new rebellion. Panic prompted the forming of more militias and more killings of slaves and free blacks. Innocent blacks were tortured into confessing to a rebellion that was never scheduled to take place. Courts tried and executed eleven blacks. There were many lynchings, in which a group of citizens unlawfully captured a person and hanged him or her without a trial.[9]

More rumors were given substance by newspaper headlines. Raleigh and Wilmington, North Carolina, were supposed to have been set on fire, and many white people murdered. Little by little, it became apparent that anxiety, and not a slave army, was responsible for the exaggerated rumors.

The Government Reacts

The governors of Virginia and North Carolina were trying to sort fact from fiction, keep people calm, and not cause too much damage to their own political careers. Governor John Floyd of Virginia, who was also a doctor, sent troops to all the towns that were sure rebellion was upon them. He began to realize that most of the hysteria was unfounded. It became his job to convince the people of his state that the danger was over, that in fact, rebellions had never even started anywhere but in Southampton County.

Floyd was worried about what the rest of the country would think about slavery in Virginia. He was even more worried that no one would lend money for much needed commercial improvement to a state that was in constant danger of slave rebellion. Though Floyd privately understood that it was the institution of slavery itself that was at fault, he could not publicize that thought.[10] He was also sure that Nat Turner was simply one of a group of religious fanatics who could, and would, rebel whenever possible. Floyd's major response was to deal as swiftly as possible with black preachers and their congregations by outlawing meetings. He believed that the problem lay with them and with free blacks and abolitionists of all religions.

Governor Montford Stokes of North Carolina came to the conclusion that no major rebellion was coming in the aftermath of the Southampton Insurrection. He regretted the suffering of the innocent blacks. Like Governor Floyd, he blamed the rebellion on "fanatics of their own complexion and other incendiaries."[11] His solution was the same as Virginia's—suppress freedom of religion and train more armies.

Meanwhile, the trials of captured rebels began. In quickly convened civil and criminal courts, the rebels

Governor John Floyd of Virginia sent troops to help suppress the rebellion, then turned to the task of convincing the people that the danger had passed.

were tried and found guilty of insurrection. On September 9, five black rebels were hanged. By that date, fourteen rebels had been tried and thirteen found guilty. Trials would continue for thirty-five other men.

Searching for Nat Turner

Notably missing from the jail in Jerusalem was Nat Turner himself. Governor Floyd offered a reward of five hundred dollars to anyone who captured and delivered Nat Turner to the county jail. A notice was

---

SOURCE DOCUMENT

WHEREAS THE SLAVE NAT, OTHERWISE CALLED NAT TURNER, THE CONTRIVER AND LEADER OF THE LATE INSURRECTION IN SOUTHAMPTON, IS STILL GOING AT LARGE: THEREFORE I, JOHN FLOYD, GOVERNOR OF THE COMMONWEALTH OF VIRGINIA, HAVE THOUGHT PROPER, AND HEREBY OFFER A REWARD OF FIVE HUNDRED DOLLARS TO ANY PERSON OR PERSONS WHO WILL APPREHEND AND CONVEY TO THE JAIL AT SOUTHAMPTON COUNTY, THE SAID SLAVE NAT: AND I DO MOREOVER REQUIRE ALL OFFICERS CIVIL AND MILITARY, AND EXHORT THE GOOD PEOPLE OF THE COMMONWEALTH TO USE THEIR BEST ENDEAVORS TO CAUSE THE SAID FUGITIVE TO BE APPREHENDED THAT HE MAY BE DEALT WITH AS THE LAW DIRECTS.[12]

In an effort to bring the leader of the rebellion to justice, Governor Floyd issued this proclamation, calling for Turner's capture and offering a reward to the person who successfully brought the rebel leader into custody.

published on September 17 that included a description of Nat Turner on the reverse side. William Parker, one of the lawyers who defended the rebels, interviewed people who had known Turner for a long time in order to be able to describe him well. The description was very detailed, including, "A scar on one of his temples produced by the kick of a mule—also one on the back of his neck by a bite—a large knot on one of the bones of his right arm near the wrist produced by a blow."[13]

The search for the elusive rebel leader continued. No one would feel comfortable until Nat Turner was in custody.

THE CAPTURE AND TRIAL OF NAT TURNER

Nat Turner left Cabin Pond on the afternoon of August 24. Finally realizing he was alone, he went into swampland. He came out that night and went to the Travis farm, which was deserted. He took some food and decided not to go back into the woods. There, the militia was wandering about, ready to shoot anything that moved. Turner dashed straight across meadows and cotton fields, where no one would expect him to be. In one field, he saw some fence rails, piled up. He dug a hole under the rails and hid inside it.[1]

Nat Turner Remains in Hiding

Nat Turner lived in his dug-out hole for six full weeks. He went out at night to drink water from a pond, but quickly came back and lay nearly motionless in his hole all day long. When he became very hungry, he began going to nearby farms at night to steal food.

Over time, it became harder for him to stay shut up in the hole, and he began to walk around the woods for many hours at night. One night, he returned to his hole and saw a dog there, sniffing at meat Turner had stored. Several nights later, the dog came back with two slaves. The dog barked and Turner emerged from the hole. The slaves barely recognized him. The rebel leader's clothes were in rags and he was thin and dirty. Though Turner begged them not to tell anyone they had seen him, he knew that the slaves, who ran away, frightened, would betray him.[2]

The Capture of Nat Turner

When word got out that Nat Turner was alive and right under their noses in Southampton County, more volunteer militia troops were organized. Armed white men surged through the fields and pastures, looking for Turner. There was a reward at stake—and some fame, too. Turner left his hideout and, barely ahead of armed groups of men, ran through the countryside. He could not get out of Southampton County. Cavalry men were stationed at all the borders. He could hear the bloodhounds howling as he hid by day and ran by night. Turner said,

> I . . . was pursued almost incessantly until I was taken a fortnight afterwards by Mr. Benjamin Phipps, in a little hole I had dug out with my sword, for the purpose of concealment, under the top of a fallen tree. On Mr. Phipps' discovering the place of my concealment, he cocked his gun and aimed at me. I requested him not to shoot and I would give up, upon which he demanded my sword.[3]

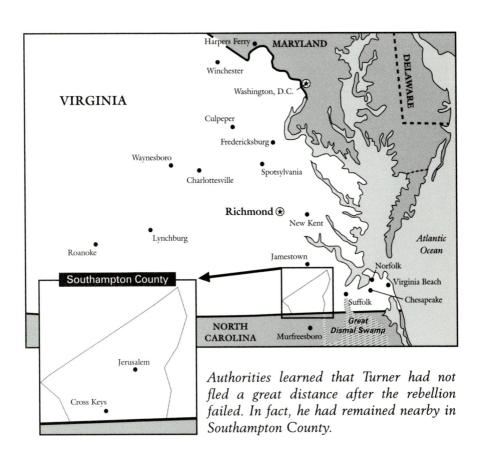

MARYLAND

DELAWARE

Harpers Ferry

Winchester

Washington, D.C.

VIRGINIA

Culpeper

Fredericksburg

Waynesboro

Spotsylvania

Charlottesville

Richmond ⊛

New Kent

Lynchburg

Atlantic
Ocean

Roanoke

Jamestown

Norfolk

Southampton County

Virginia Beach

Suffolk

Chesapeake

NORTH
CAROLINA

Murfreesboro

Great
Dismal Swamp

Jerusalem

Cross Keys

*Authorities learned that Turner had not
fled a great distance after the rebellion
failed. In fact, he had remained nearby in
Southampton County.*

Benjamin Phipps, a farmer, had not been looking for Nat Turner. He was resting before continuing his walk home when he noticed some brush moving by a broken tree limb. He picked up his shotgun and walked toward the tree. Suddenly, a head appeared from under the tree. It belonged to thin, bedraggled Nat Turner.[4]

When Turner handed over his sword and his hands were tied, Phipps fired his shotgun in the air, attracting a crowd of people. The starved-looking man was taken to Peter Edwards's plantation as the crowd grew larger. Riders spurred their horses to Jerusalem to yell out the news. Nat Turner was taken to Cross Keys, the tiny crossroads village near the devastated farms. The angry crowd screamed, urging Turner's captors to lynch him. Though he was whipped by his guards, local people who had been recruited quickly when Turner was spotted, Turner never cried out. The general of the rebel forces was kept in a farmhouse, watched by guards, for the night, before continuing the walk into Jerusalem.

Turner Is Put in Jail

Nat Turner arrived in Jerusalem around 1:15 P.M. He was marched across the same bridge he had hoped his rebel army would cross in triumph. He was interrogated in the courtroom by judges and several men who took notes for the Richmond *Enquirer*, the Richmond *Whig*, and the Norfolk *American Beacon*. The spit-upon prophet spoke clearly, taking full responsibility for being the leader of the rebellion. "He is a shrewd, intelligent

Nat Turner's hiding place was discovered accidentally by Benjamin Phipps many weeks after the failure of the rebellion.

fellow; he insists strongly upon the revelations which he received, as he understood them, urging him on, and pointing to this enterprize," reported the Richmond *Whig* on November 7, 1831.[5]

About the massacre—where women and children were killed as well as white men—a November 1 letter to the Richmond *Enquirer* said,

> He [Turner] says that indiscriminate massacre was not their intention after they obtained a foothold, and was resorted to in the first instance to strike terror and alarm. Women and children would afterwards have been spared, and men too who ceased to resist. . . .[6]

Another letter said that Nat Turner "is making a voluntary confession, of the motives which induced him to commence the insurrection, to Mr. Thomas B. [*sic*] Gray, who intends publishing them in pamphlet form, for the satisfaction of the public."[7]

Not much is known about Thomas R. Gray except that he was a lawyer, around sixty years of age, with a wife and no children. He was one of the three defense lawyers who came from in and around Jerusalem for the trials of the rebels. The others were William Parker and James French. Gray also owned about seventeen slaves.

Nat Turner was being kept in chains in a cell. Several of the other free blacks who were part of his army were in the jail also, and Turner found out what had happened to the rest of the men. His trusted three, who had known about his plans before anyone else— Hark, Sam, and Nelson—had been hanged on September 9. The fourth, Henry, had been killed earlier.

Turner's trial was scheduled to be held on November 5. It was already November 1.

Thomas Gray came into Turner's cell and said he wanted to write down Turner's confessions for publication. He told Turner he wanted to get the facts straight, to help the public understand why slaves would rebel in such a violent way. An unknown correspondent to the Richmond *Whig* wrote that everything about the Southampton Insurrection was "wrapt in mystery," until Nat Turner, the leader of the rebel slaves, was captured.[8]

The Confessions of Nat Turner

Turner agreed to make a full confession. Though we have no way of knowing if the language recorded in the confessions was exactly the way Nat Turner spoke, it is a very important document, because it is the only first-hand account of the rebellion. The facts seem to be correct because the things Turner says, through Thomas Gray, in the confessions match eyewitness reports and reports of Turner's words from the first interrogation on Tuesday, November 1. The confessions tell us all we really know about this intelligent man who started a bloody rebellion. Historian Stephen B. Oates wrote,

> Though Nat never said so, this would be his last opportunity to strike back at the slave world he hated, to flay it with verbal brilliance and religious prophecy. . . . Indeed, a published confession would ensure Nat a kind of immortality; it would recount his extraordinary life in his own words and on his own terms. . . .[9]

SOURCE DOCUMENT

AGREEABLE TO HIS OWN APPOINTMENT, ON THE EVENING HE WAS COMMITTED TO PRISON, WITH PERMISSION OF THE JAILER, I VISITED NAT ON TUESDAY THE 1ST NOVEMBER, WHEN, WITHOUT BEING QUESTIONED AT ALL, HE COMMENCED HIS NARRATIVE IN THE FOLLOWING WORDS:—

SIR, YOU HAVE ASKED ME TO GIVE A HISTORY OF THE MOTIVES WHICH INDUCED ME TO UNDERTAKE THE LATE INSURRECTION, AS YOU CALL IT— . . . WHICH HAS TERMINATED FATALLY TO MANY BOTH BLACK AND WHITE, AND FOR WHICH I AM ABOUT TO ATONE AT THE GALLOWS.[10]

Thomas Gray recorded Nat Turner's confessions while Turner was in jail. This is the only firsthand account that actually remains of the rebellion.

The Trial of the Rebel Leader

At the trial, there were only prosecution witnesses. Thomas Gray's manuscript of the confessions was read to the court. Nat Turner pleaded not guilty. Judge Jeremiah Cobb pronounced the sentence of the court, in the following words: "Nat Turner! Stand up. Have you any thing to say why sentence of death should not be pronounced against you? *Answer.* I have not. I have made a full confession to Mr. Gray, and I have nothing more to say."[11]

Judge Cobb then went on to talk about the horrible crime of which Turner was convicted. The judge believed he had been "led away by fanaticism." He said that, if that were so, he pitied Turner, but had no choice but to pass the sentence of the court:

> The judgment of the court is, that you be taken hence to the jail from whence you came, thence to the place of execution, and on Friday next, between the hours of 10 A.M. and 2 P.M. be hung by the neck until you are dead! dead! dead! and may the Lord have mercy upon your soul.[12]

Nat Turner was hanged on November 11, 1831, in front of a huge crowd. When asked if he had anything he wanted to say, Turner simply replied, "I'm ready."[13]

9

REVENGE OF THE SOUTH

The revenge of white Southerners against the slave rebels did not end with the hanging of Nat Turner. Unruly militia units and vigilantes had already taken revenge against innocent and free blacks as well as the rebels. Now it was the state's turn. Virginia would get even with the rebels through legislation. As had occurred after all previous slave rebellions, the result was tougher slave codes, which hoped to prevent future uprisings by taking away even more freedom from the slaves.

Debates on Slavery

However, after the Turner Rebellion, there were several months during which the continuation of slavery was debated fiercely in Virginia. The largest number of petitions sent to the Virginia legislature focused on the problem of population size. In many counties in 1831, blacks outnumbered whites. Freeing all slaves seemed dangerous to Virginians. After all, it was free slaves who had, along with Northern abolitionists, caused all the trouble by encouraging slaves to revolt. This, as always among slaveholders, was a comfortable position.

This letter to North Carolina Governor Montford
Stokes informed him of the imprisonment, trial, and
execution of some slaves in Sampson and Dublin
counties as a result of rumors of slave rebellion.

Many thought the solution was to free the slaves gradually. This was to be coupled with colonization—sending blacks to another country. In January and February 1832, the Virginia legislature began open discussions on the problem of slavery. Called the Virginia Debate on Slavery, these discussions took place in the newspapers as well as the legislature. Governor Floyd, who privately felt that slavery had to end in Virginia, did not talk about abolition in his speeches. Instead, he called for more sanctions, more militia, and more caution.[1] He also blamed black preachers and outside agitators for the conditions leading up to the rebellion.

Notably absent were the voices of Virginians who saw slavery as an institution that was rotten at the center and lacked any excuse for existence. Southerners would leave that argument to the abolitionists. Some slave owners still made claims for the basic happiness of Virginia slaves.

"I will not discuss the abstract question of the right of slavery: but I will say that the slaves of Va. are as happy a laboring class as exists upon the habitable globe," said James Ghalson, a legislative representative of Brunswick County, Virginia.[2] He went on to say that Nat Turner was an isolated incident—a religious fanatic. He could only gather a few slaves, out of hundreds in his path, to join his rebellion.

General William H. Brodnax, whose troops helped end the rebellion, had a different opinion, "That *slavery in Virginia is an evil* . . . it would be idle . . . for any human being to doubt or deny."[3] Still, Brodnax

SOURCE DOCUMENT

IN THE DEBATE OF THE VIRGINIA LEGISLATURE, NO
SPEAKER INSINUATED EVEN, WE BELIEVE, THAT THE SLAVES
IN VIRGINIA WERE NOT TREATED KINDLY; AND ALL, TOO,
AGREE THAT THEY WERE MOST ABUNDANTLY FED; AND WE
HAVE NO DOUBT THAT THEY FORM THE HAPPIEST PORTION
OF OUR SOCIETY. A MERRIER BEING DOES NOT EXIST ON
THE FACE OF THE GLOBE, THAN THE NEGRO SLAVE OF THE
U. STATES.[4]

During the Virginia debates on slavery after Nat Turner's rebellion, few Southerners dared to speak against the peculiar institution. In fact, as this review of the debates illustrates, most continued to defend slavery strongly.

believed "That no emancipation of slaves should ever be tolerated, unaccompanied by their immediate removal from among us."[5] Furthermore, Brodnax believed, private property, which slaves were considered, had to be recognized and no slave could be legally taken away without the owner's consent.

One of the few antislavery voices in the South belonged to James McDowell, a delegate from Rockbridge County, Virginia. He disagreed that the Southampton Insurrection was "a petty affair."[6] He believed slaveholders would constantly fear that a "Nat Turner might be in every family, that the same bloody deed could be acted over at any time and in any place. . . ."[7]

After Nat Turner's rebellion, many Southerners decided it was too dangerous to allow black slaves to preach to other blacks. This bill was designed to prevent blacks from preaching.

The Virginia debates finally ended in confusion over methods for gradual emancipation. All that happened was the passage of more slave codes. Open debate ended. Black preachers were prohibited from speaking at churches or gatherings. All over the South, even tighter codes against teaching blacks to read and write were enforced.

Pretty soon talk of any kind of emancipation ceased. Arguments for slavery as a benefit to society increased. History was supposed to favor slavery, according to the proslavery forces. The ever-ready argument of racial inferiority became even further entrenched. Despite the strengthening of the institution of slavery, however, antislavery forces were still alive, gaining in strength every day.

·10·

ABOLITIONISTS AND CIVIL WAR

Despite the fierce reprisals and stiffer slave codes, slaves were making their way to the North and to freedom. There, able to get an education, many became increasingly vocal members of the abolitionist movement. David Walker's *Appeal*, which Nat Turner might have read or known about, turned the corner toward a more militant outcry against slavery. William Lloyd Garrison, who disliked the violence of Nat Turner's Southampton Insurrection, believed the rebellion was inevitable and that such events would happen again.

Nat Turner Inspires the Abolition Movement

The New York *Daily Sentinel*, even before Nat Turner was captured, used strong editorials about the Southampton Insurrection in order to denounce slavery: ". . . almost all the accounts concur in stating that they expected to emancipate themselves, and they no doubt thought that their only hope of doing so was to put to death, indiscriminately, the whole race of those who held them in bondage."[1] The *Sentinel* went on

William Lloyd Garrison, the prominent abolitionist and publisher of The Liberator, *was upset by the violence of Turner's rebellion. However, he felt such bloody revolts would occur again if slavery were not abolished immediately.*

SOURCE DOCUMENT

THE NEWS FROM THE SOUTH IS GLORIOUS. GENERAL NAT IS A BENEFACTOR OF HIS RACE. THE SOUTHAMPTON MASSACRE IS AN AUSPICIOUS ERA FOR THE AFRICAN. THE BLOOD OF THE MEN, WOMEN AND CHILDREN SHED BY THE SWORD AND THE AXE IN THE HAND OF THE NEGRO IS A JUST RETURN FOR THE DROPS WHICH HAVE FOLLOWED THE MASTER'S LASH.[2]

Northern abolitionists reacted to news of Turner's rebellion positively. Many thought it was a big step toward abolishing slavery in the South. This statement of a Northern abolitionist was recorded by F. G. Fontaine in his 1861 history of the abolition movement.

to say that, although the chances of the rebellion's succeeding "were absurd . . . Would the blacks have attempted their foolish project, if they had possessed even the mere rudiments of a common education? Never." The fault lay with the slave owners, who kept education from their slaves:

Virginia—yes, the state which gave birth to the immortal Jefferson, the author of the declaration that declares that *all* men are born *free and equal*—that declaration which no slaveholder dare dispute the truth of—Virginia! at the last session of its legislature, passed a law making it penal [illegal] for a slaveholder to teach his own slaves to read and write![3]

In 1843, Henry H. Garnet, a former slave who had escaped to Buffalo, New York, delivered a speech in which he reminded his listeners of Nat Turner and urged rebellion. Henry Biff wrote about Nat Turner and Denmark Vesey in biographies and abolitionist songs:

I hear the voice of Turner, of Turner, of Turner,
I hear the voice of Turner, for Liberty or Death!
Oh! set the captive free, set him free, set him free,
Oh! set the captive free from his chains.[4]

In 1850, a Fugitive Slave Law was passed, in order to capture runaway slaves more easily. This was part of the Compromise of 1850, which let California into the Union as a free state, while allowing the new territories of Utah and New Mexico to choose whether

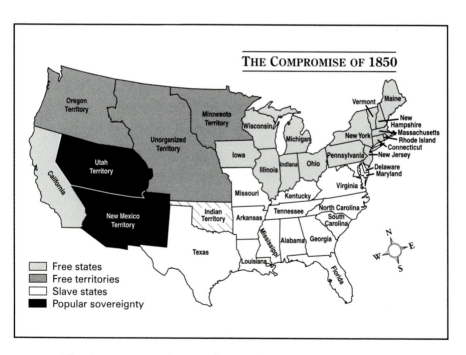

THE COMPROMISE OF 1850

Free states
Free territories
Slave states
Popular sovereignty

The Compromise of 1850, designed to ease tensions between proslavery and antislavery forces, caused even worse friction between the North and the South.

The Fugitive Slave Act of 1850, part of the Compromise of 1850, made it easier for slave owners to have escaped slaves returned to them. This poster shows slaves running from slave catchers.

to be slave states or free (a concept called popular sovereignty). The compromise, designed to keep the United States together in the face of increasing hostility between proslavery and antislavery forces, did not please Northern abolitionists.

In 1854, a riot occurred at the federal courthouse in Boston when Anthony Burns, a fugitive slave, was put on trial. Although the decision went against Burns and he was returned to his master in the South, the trial and others like it fueled the fires of abolition. The end of slavery was in sight.

Harpers Ferry

By 1859, the abolition movement was stronger than ever. One abolitionist, following in Nat Turner's footsteps, tried to end slavery in a violent way. Militant abolitionist John Brown led an unsuccessful raid at Harpers Ferry, Virginia (now in West Virginia), and became the symbol that the abolition movement needed. With a small force of white and black abolitionists, Brown attacked the town, hoping to capture its arsenal. He intended to give weapons to the slaves of the area, whom he believed would rise up in rebellion and end slavery once and for all. Brown's raid was put down by the United States military, and Brown himself was hanged. Like Nat Turner, however, he became a symbol of the antislavery movement and an inspiration to abolitionists everywhere.

Thomas Wentworth Higginson, a noted historian and abolitionist who was a friend of John Brown's, wrote an essay on Nat Turner. In it, he compared the courage and dignity of Brown and Turner, referring to Nat Turner as a genuine hero. Higginson admired Turner for his intelligence, particularly in having evaded capture for "five weary weeks and six days."[5]

A Nation Divided

By now, tensions were higher than ever between the North and the South. Abraham Lincoln was elected president in 1860, the preferred candidate of the abolitionists. In response, Southern states, led by South Carolina, began to leave the Union. In April 1861, the

Militant abolitionist John Brown led a failed slave rebellion in Harpers Ferry, Virginia, in 1859. Like Nat Turner, he became a hero to antislavery Northerners and was hated by proslavery Southerners.

Civil War began. Though the war came about because of the South's wish to start its own government—the Confederacy—where the states were supreme, the issue of slavery fueled the division as the Confederates continued to fight.

In 1862, when it was clear that President Abraham Lincoln would soon deliver a proclamation freeing the slaves held by the rebelling Southern states, the Richmond *Enquirer* called the abolition of slavery an insurrection in itself. Recalling the massacre of women and children in the Turner Rebellion, the paper dramatically said that Lincoln, by the proclamation, would be condoning butchery: "What shall we call him?—coward? assassin? savage? . . . Shall we consider these all embodied in the word 'fiend!' . . . Lincoln, the Fiend."[6]

But, fiend or not, Lincoln declared slavery to be over in the rebelling states on January 1, 1863. Because he could not enforce the proclamation, which applied only to those states no longer in the Union, it took the victory of Northern forces to end slavery officially. This occurred through the passage of the Thirteenth Amendment to the United States Constitution in 1865.

Nat Turner Remembered

After the Civil War, Nat Turner remained a folk hero among blacks, and several black historians wrote essays about him. Turner's confessions were reprinted in 1881, and a debate on whether a statue should be built of John Brown or Nat Turner went on in two black newspapers. Frederick Douglass, Jr., editor of the

Washington National Leader, suggested building a statue of John Brown. An editor at the *New York Age* believed that Nat Turner was a better choice:

> Nat Turner was a black hero. He preferred death to slavery. He ought to have a monument. White men care nothing for his memory. We should cherish it. It is quite remarkable that whenever colored men move that somebody's memory be perpetuated, that somebody's memory is always a white man's.[7]

This debate actually indicated the wave of the future in black-white relations. Abolitionists were, or tried to be, color-blind. Reconstruction, which tried to reorganize the Southern states that had seceded in a manner that would make both races receive equal treatment, failed miserably. Carpetbaggers, people

SOURCE DOCUMENT

NAT TURNER IS NOT DEAD. HE LIVES IN THE HEARTS OF THOSE WHO LOVE FREEDOM AND LIBERTY. THOUGH HIS BODY IS RESTING IN A QUIET BURYING GROUND, PLACED THERE BY THOSE WHO LOVE SLAVERY, NOT FREEDOM. HE WAS HANGED AND MURDERED BECAUSE HE DARED TO SPEAK IN BEHALF OF LIBERTY AND FOR NO OTHER CAUSE WAS HE MURDERED. NAT TURNER, WHOSE SOUL NOW LINGERS IN THE HEAVENS, SPEAKS IN HISTORIC TRUTHS OF THE NOBLE DEAD.[8]

By the late 1800s, Nat Turner was being viewed as a hero in many black communities. This 1889 lecture by George H. Burks shows the blacks' attitude toward Turner's rebellion.

who came to the South from the North and took advantage of a society in chaos to make money for themselves, were one problem. The federal government also did not supply enough structure to help with the economic transition. Ultimately, Southerners continued to treat blacks violently and refused to respect their newly won civil rights. Because of the continuing discrimination against blacks, a new, racially conscious attitude emerged among black intellectuals.

At the same time, apologies for slavery began appearing again in white histories. By the 1900s, Nat Turner was rarely mentioned except in the memories of Southern blacks. During Negro History Week, Southern black children celebrated Nat Turner as a great hero, and sang this song:

> *Well you can be milk-white*
> *and just as rich as cream*
> *And buy a solid gold carriage*
> *with a four-horse team*
> *But you caint keep the world*
> *from movering round*
> *Or stop Old Nat Turner from*
> *gaining ground.*[9]

11

THE LEGACY

It was not until the 1967 publication of famous novelist William Styron's *The Confessions of Nat Turner* that Nat Turner once again became a controversial figure. Though he had always been a hero in the folk tradition of the black South, and probably lived on just below the surface of relations between blacks and whites, he was a small paragraph in history books. Styron changed all that.

Styron's book on Nat Turner was eagerly anticipated by both black and white historians and writers. *The Confessions of Nat Turner* was glowingly reviewed by major reviewers—all of whom were white. It became a best-seller and won the Pulitzer Prize.[1]

During the 1960s, in reaction to the post–Civil War segregation, there was much racial tension and civil rights activism. This probably helped the book and led to increased interest. It also intensified the backlash. If the white establishment liked the book very much, the black community hated it twice as much. Black critics said so in definite terms, and again debates raged, this time in the literary press.

There were three major objections to Styron's portrait of Nat Turner. One was that it was not true to the

★ 98 ★

history of slavery and the way blacks think—then or now. It was not even true to the small amount of historical fact known about Nat Turner himself. The real Nat Turner had a wife and two children. His wife, Cherry, was whipped to force her to give up the papers he had left for her. It is also presumed that he spared the farm of Giles Reese, on the rebel path, because his wife and children lived there. In his book, Styron turned Nat Turner from a rebel hero to a deluded fanatic by making him a single man who had romantic fantasies about white women. "Instead of the man of meditation who fasted and prayed to become the Moses of his people, instead of the good shepherd . . . both black and white men of the gospel will find here a black man who really wants to marry somebody's white sister. . . ." wrote critic Albert Murray.[2]

The third objection had to do with language and style. Styron's Nat Turner talks like an essay, not like a man, said several writers. Black writers also felt that the religious and mystical beliefs that brought Nat Turner to the edge of revolution were never understood or fulfilled in Styron's book.

Whatever the truth of the various good and bad reviews might have been, the result of the publication of Styron's novel was a revived Nat Turner in American history. It also showed that division between the races remains, even many years after the end of slavery.

Nat Turner, whose rebellion was so very bloody, seems not to have been a violent man by choice. The excesses of slavery caused the excesses of his rebellion.

Ossie Davis, a famous black writer, wrote in 1968,

Deep down inside, even when we didn't know his name, Nat Turner was always alive. Nat, by whatever name we called him, or dreamed of him, or told stories about him, Nat was our secret weapon, our ace in the hole, our private consciousness of manhood kept strictly between us.[3]

Biographer Lamont H. Yeakey wrote,

This slave rebellion catalyzed the beginning of the abolitionist movement in the United States. Because Turner's motive was a desire for liberty, he may be regarded as cast in the same mold as the American patriots who fought the Revolutionary War and as other freedom-loving men. Not less than Patrick Henry, Turner too believed that "give me liberty or give me death" must be man's guiding philosophy of life.[4]

Though slavery ended many years ago, racial hostility and tensions continue. Turner's dream of racial equality and freedom is still alive today, as the struggle for equal rights and an end to racial discrimination goes on.

★ TIMELINE ★

1619—First black slaves brought to mainland North America in Jamestown, Virginia.

1799—Nat Turner's mother, Nancy, bought at auction by Benjamin Turner.

1800—Nat Turner is born in Southampton County, Virginia; Gabriel Prosser and coconspirators are executed for insurrection.

1821—Turner runs away; Returns a month later.

1822—Turner marries Cherry, a slave girl owned by Benjamin Turner; Nat Turner sold to Thomas Moore; Denmark Vesey conspiracy discovered in Charleston, South Carolina.

1825—Turner claims he experiences a vision.

1828—*May 12*: Turner has a vision telling him to take on Christ's yoke and "fight against the serpent."

1829—David Walker's *Appeal* is published.

1831—*January 1*: First issue of *The Liberator* is published by William Lloyd Garrison.

February: Eclipse of the sun signals rebellion to Turner.

April: Virginia legislature makes it a felony to teach blacks and slaves to read and write.

July 4: Chosen date for insurrection; Turner is sick.

August 13: Turner sees a new sign for rebellion as the sun looks greenish.

August 21: Turner meets with friends to plan rebellion.

August 22: Rebellion begins before dawn; Joseph Travis and family killed; By afternoon, "Battle of Parker's field" takes place; Rebels break apart.

August 23: Rebels try to attack Blunt farm and are fired on; Turner waits alone at Cabin Pond.

August 23–26: Whites take revenge by massacring Southampton blacks.

August 31: Trials of rebels begin.

September 4: Execution of rebels begins.

October 30: Nat Turner captured by Benjamin Phipps.

November 1–3: Thomas Gray listens to and writes *The Confessions of Nat Turner*.

November 5: Trial of Nat Turner takes place.

November 11: Execution of Nat Turner carried out in Jerusalem.

1832—*January*: Virginia Debate on Slavery takes place.

March: Open debate over; Laws are made forbidding blacks to preach; Slave codes are further tightened.

★ CHAPTER NOTES ★

Chapter 1. Insurrection

1. Quoted in Eric Foner, ed., *Nat Turner: Great Lives Observed* (New Jersey: Prentice-Hall, Inc., 1971), p. 83.

2. Ibid., p. 14.

Chapter 2. The Peculiar Institution

1. Quoted in Leslie H. Fishel, Jr., and Benjamin Quarles, eds., *The Negro American: A Documentary History* (Illinois: Scott, Foresman and Company, 1967), p. 19.

2. Ibid.

3. Ibid., p. 20.

4. Alexis de Tocqueville, *Democracy in America*, trans. Henry Reeves (London: 1838), vol. 2, pp. 214–217.

5. Fishel and Quarles, p. 5.

6. Ibid., p. 21.

7. Quoted in Merrill Jensen, ed., *American Colonial Documents to 1776* (London: Eyre and Spottiswoode, Otd., 1955), vol. 9, pp. 491–493.

8. Fishel, p. 37.

9. Ibid., p. 72.

10. Ibid., p. 82.

11. Ibid., p. 85.

Chapter 3. Who Was Nat Turner?

1. Stephen B. Oates, *The Fires of Jubilee: Nat Turner's Fierce Rebellion* (New York: Harper & Row, 1975), p. 12.

2. Quoted in John B. Duff and Peter M. Mitchell, eds., *The Nat Turner Rebellion: The Historical Event and the Modern Controversy* (New York: Harper & Row, 1971), p. 15.

3. Ibid., p. 16.

4. Ibid.

5. Ibid., p. 17.

6. Leslie H. Fishel, Jr., and Benjamin Quarles, eds., *The Negro American: A Documentary History* (Illinois: Scott, Foresman and Company, 1967), p. 111.

7. Duff and Mitchell, p. 16.

8. Ibid., p. 18.

9. Ibid.

10. Ibid., p. 19.

11. Oates, p. 48.

12. Ibid.

Chapter 4. Leading Up to Nat Turner

1. Stephen B. Oates, *The Fires of Jubilee: Nat Turner's Fierce Rebellion* (New York: Harper & Row, 1975), p. 17.

2. Ibid., p. 51.

3. Eric Foner, ed., *Nat Turner: Great Lives Observed* (New Jersey: Prentice-Hall, Inc., 1971), p. 6.

4. Ibid., p. 80.

Chapter 5. The Stage Is Set

1. Quoted in John B. Duff and Peter M. Mitchell, eds., *The Nat Turner Rebellion: The Historical Event and the Modern Controversy* (New York: Harper & Row, 1971), p. 19.

2. Ibid.

3. Stephen B. Oates, *The Fires of Jubilee: Nat Turner's Fierce Rebellion* (New York: Harper & Row, 1975), p. 54.

4. Ibid., p. 27.

5. Ibid., p. 66.

6. Ibid., p. 67.

Chapter 6. The Southampton Insurrection

1. Quoted in John B. Duff and Peter M. Mitchell, eds., *The Nat Turner Rebellion: The Historical Event and the Modern Controversy* (New York: Harper & Row, 1971), pp. 21–22.

2. Stephen B. Oates, *The Fires of Jubilee: Nat Turner's Fierce Rebellion* (New York: Harper & Row, 1975), p. 92.

3. Ibid., p. 95.

4. Ibid., p. 101.

5. Duff and Mitchell, p. 23.

6. Ibid., p. 24.

Chapter 7. Swift Reprisal

1. Eric Foner, ed., *Nat Turner: Great Lives Observed* (New Jersey: Prentice-Hall, Inc., 1971), pp. 15–16.

2. Quoted in Ibid., p. 5.

3. Ibid.

4. Public Broadcasting Service, "The Richmond *Enquirer* on Nat Turner's Rebellion," *Africans in America*, n.d., <http://www.pbs.org/wgbh/aia/part3/3h499.html> (August 5, 1999).

5. Foner, p. 19.

6. Ibid., p. 27.

7. Ibid.

8. Ibid., p. 29.

9. Stephen B. Oates, *The Fires of Jubilee: Nat Turner's Fierce Rebellion* (New York: Harper & Row, 1975), p. 113.

10. Foner, pp. 99–104.

11. Oates, p. 123.

12. *The Governor's Proclamation of a Reward for the Capture of Nat Turner*, n.d., <http://www/melanet.com/nat/nat_proc.html> (August 5, 1999).

13. Oates, p. 130.

Chapter 8. The Capture and Trial of Nat Turner

1. Quoted in John B. Duff and Peter M. Mitchell, eds., *The Nat Turner Rebellion: The Historical Event and the Modern Controversy* (New York: Harper & Row, 1971), p. 25.

2. Ibid.

3. Ibid.

4. Ibid.

5. Quoted in Eric Foner, ed., *Nat Turner: Great Lives Observed* (New Jersey: Prentice-Hall, Inc., 1971), pp. 31–32.

6. Ibid., p. 33.

7. Ibid.

8. Stephen B. Oates, *The Fires of Jubilee: Nat Turner's Fierce Rebellion* (New York: HarperPerennial, 1990), p. 121.

9. Ibid.

10. "History of Motives," *The Confessions of Nat Turner*, n.d., <http://odur.let.rug.nl/~usa/D/1826-1850/slavery/confes02.htm> (August 5, 1999).

11. Duff and Mitchell, p. 28.

12. Ibid.

13. Ibid., p. 29.

Chapter 9. Revenge of the South

1. Eric Foner, ed., *Nat Turner: Great Lives Observed* (New Jersey: Prentice-Hall, Inc., 1971), p. 8.

2. Quoted in Ibid., p. 107.

3. Ibid., p. 109.

4. Thomas R. Dew, "Review of the Debate in the Virginia Legislature of 1831 and 1832," *Great Issues in American History*, ed. Richard Hofstadter (New York: Vintage Books, 1958), vol. 2, p. 318.

5. Foner, p. 110.

6. Ibid., p. 112.

7. Ibid., p. 113.

Chapter 10. Abolitionists and Civil War

1. Quoted in Eric Foner, ed., *Nat Turner: Great Lives Observed* (New Jersey: Prentice-Hall, Inc., 1971), p. 77.

2. Library of Congress, *American Memory*, n.d., <http://memory.loc.gov/> (August 5, 1999).

3. Foner, p. 77.

4. Henry Bibb, *Slave Insurrection in Southampton County, Va., Headed by Nat Turner* (New York: 1850), p. 127.

5. Thomas Wentworth Higginson, "Nat Turner's Insurrection," *Atlantic Monthly*, vol. 8, August 1861, pp. 173–187.

6. Quoted in Foner, p. 140.

7. "John Brown and Nat Turner," *The New York Age*, January 12, 1889.

8. Library of Congress, *American Memory*.

9. Albert Murray, "A Troublesome Property," *The New Leader*, December 4, 1967, pp. 18–21.

Chapter 11. The Legacy

1. John B. Duff and Peter M. Mitchell, eds., *The Nat Turner Rebellion: The Historical Event and the Modern Controversy* (New York: Harper & Row, 1971), p. 116.

2. Albert Murray, "A Troublesome Property," *The New Leader*, December 4, 1967, pp. 18–21.

3. Ossie Davis, "Nat Turner: Hero Reclaimed," *Freedomways Magazine*, vol. 8, no. 3, Summer 1968, p. 231.

4. Lamont H. Yeakey, "N. Turner," *The McGraw-Hill Encyclopedia of World Biography* (New York: McGraw Hill, 1973), vol. 11, p. 33.

★ FURTHER READING ★

Books

Altman, Linda Jacobs. *Slavery and Abolition in American History*. Berkeley Heights, N.J.: Enslow Publishers, Inc., 1999.

Bisson, Terry. *Nat Turner: Slave Revolt Leader*. New York: Chelsea House Publishers, 1995.

Oates, Stephen B. *The Fires of Jubilee: Nat Turner's Fierce Rebellion*. New York: Harper & Row, 1975.

Stein, R. Conrad. *John Brown's Raid on Harpers Ferry in American History*. Berkeley Heights, N.J.: Enslow Publishers, Inc., 1999.

Styron, William. *The Confessions of Nat Turner*. New York: Random House, 1967.

Internet Addresses

The Confessions of Nat Turner. n.d. <http://odur.let.rug.nl/~usa/D/1826-1850/slavery/confes02.htm> (August 5, 1999).

Goldman, Steve. *Southampton Slave Revolt.* n.d. <http://www.historybuff.com/library/refslave.html> (August 5, 1999).

Library of Congress. *American Memory.* n.d. <http://memory.loc.gov/> (August 5, 1999).

Public Broadcasting Service. "The Richmond *Enquirer* on Nat Turner's Rebellion." *Africans in America.* n.d. <http://www.pbs.org/wgbh/aia/part3/3h499.html> (August 5, 1999).

★ INDEX ★